HERITAGE BRITAIN

Published by VisitBritain Publishing, Thames Tower, Blacks Road, London W6 9EL

First published 2007

© British Tourist Authority (trading as VisitBritain) 2007

ISBN
978 0 7095 8398 1
Product code: IMAGES03

A CIP catalogue record for this book is available from the British Library.

The information contained in this publication has been published in good faith on the basis of information submitted
to VisitBritain and is believed to be correct at time of going to press. Nevertheless, VisitBritain regrets that it cannot
guarantee complete accuracy and all liability for loss, disappointment, negligence or other damages caused by reliance
on the information contained in this publication, is hereby excluded.

All the photographs in *Heritage Britain* were selected from VisitBritain's official online image library, Britain on View.

Editorial and design by Indigo 3 Publishing for VisitBritain Publishing.
Reprographics by CTT Limited.
Printed and bound in Dubai by Oriental Press.

Front cover: Studley Royal Water Garden by Richard Watson

HERITAGE BRITAIN

HERITAGE BRITAIN

Heritage Britain captures the extraordinary diversity of Britain's rich history – a history that encompasses prehistoric myth and Arthurian legend, Elizabethan elegance and Victorian opulence; a history that tells its story through majestic palaces and atmospheric ruins, stately gardens and magnificent cathedrals.

Journeying from the Standing Stones of Callanish to the imposing fortresses of the Welsh coast, via stately gardens and the tranquil courtyards of Oxford and Cambridge, *Heritage Britain* gives a fascinating glimpse into the history of a nation shaped by generations of Britons from the Stone Age to the present day.

Taken from Britain on View, VisitBritain's own image library,
the stunning selection of photographs in this book provides
a unique visual portrait of the history of a nation.
Heritage Britain also includes a useful gazetteer of visitor
information and contact details for many of the places
and destinations featured.

*The stately
homes of England,
How beautiful
they stand,
Amidst their tall
ancestral trees,
O'er all the
pleasant land!*

FELICIA HEMENS

p22 & 23 Hampton Court Palace , Surrey

Scous : Henri: Quart : coy : Henri: Quint : Henri: Sext :

For a man's house is his castle,
et domus sua cuique est tutissimum refugium
[and each man's home is his safest refuge]

SIR EDWARD COKE

p31 Rockingham Castle, Leicestershire
p32~33 Harlech Castle, Gwynedd
p34 Blenheim Palace, Oxfordshire

HERITAGE BRITAIN

What is a church?
— Our honest sexton tells,
'Tis a tall building,
with a tower and bells.'

GEORGE CRABBE

*The many great gardens of the world,
of literature and poetry, of painting
and music, of religion and architecture,
all make the point as clear as possible:
the soul cannot thrive in the absence
of a garden. If you don't want a paradise,
you are not human, and if you are not
human, you do not have a soul.*

SIR THOMAS MORE

p62~63 Rutland Water, Rutland
p64~65 Peak District, Derbyshire

73

I wonder whether anybody
does anything at Oxford but dream
and remember, the place is so beautiful.
One almost expects the people to sing
instead of speaking. It is all like an opera.

WILLIAM BUTLER YEATS

*Somehow the air seems to dance
differently here, executing a perfect
back-flip into the arms of the
short-cropped hillsides, gliding
in sequinned splendour and perfect
three-four time across the machair.*

ALIX BROWN

The Pavilion
Cost a million
As a monument to Art
And the wits here
Say it sits here
Like an Oriental tart!

NOEL COWARD

Oh! who can ever be tired of Bath?

JANE AUSTEN

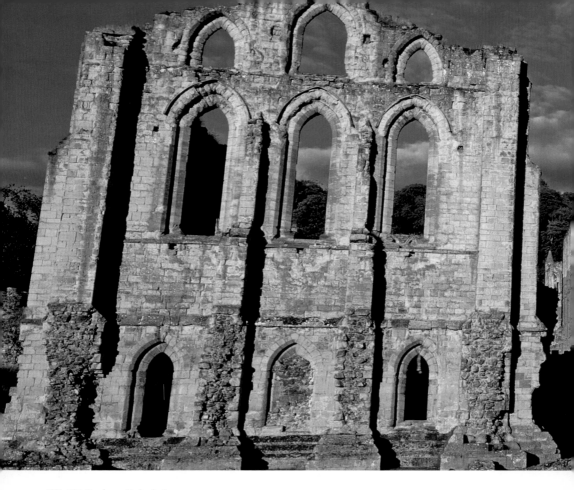

With the odd ancientry of Chester we were much amused, it renders this city perfectly unique.

ANNE SEWARD

HERITAGE BRITAIN

113

Gazetteer

Alnwick Castle (pp14-15)
The Estate Offices, Alnwick Castle, Alnwick,
Northumberland, NE66 1NQ
T: 01665 511100
W: www.alnwickcastle.com

Anglesey Abbey, Gardens and Lode Mill
(pp84-85)
Quy Road, Lode, Cambridge,
Cambridgeshire, CB5 9EJ
T: 01223 810080

Blenheim Palace (pp34-35)
Woodstock, Oxfordshire OX20 1PX
T: 01993 811091
W: www.blenheimpalace.com

Blickling Hall (pp98-99)
Blickling, Norwich, Norfolk NR11 6NF
T: 01263 738030
W: www.nationaltrust.org.uk

Bodiam Castle (pp24-25)
Bodiam, Robertsbridge, East Sussex TN32 5UA
T: 01580 830436
W: www.nationaltrust.org.uk

Burghley House (pp52-53)
The House Office, Burghley House, Stamford,
Lincolnshire PE9 3JY
T: 01780 752451 W: www.burghley.co.uk

Calanais Standing Stones Visitor Centre
(pp112-113)
Callanish, Isle of Lewis, Western Isle HS2 9DY
T: 01851 621422
W: www.calanaisvisitorcentre.co.uk

Canterbury Cathedral (pp72-73)
The Precincts, Canterbury, Kent, CT1 2EH
T: 01227 762862
W: www.canterbury-cathedral.org

Chatsworth House (pp12-13)
Chatsworth, Bakewell, Derbyshire DE45 1PP
T: 01246 582204
W: www.chatsworth.org

Chirk Castle (pp56-57)
Chirk, Wrexham LL41 5AF
T: 016914 777701
W: www.nationaltrust.org.uk

Dolwyddelan Castle (pp18-19)
Dolwyddelan, Conwy LL25 0EJ
T: 02920 500200

Dunfermline Palace and Abbey (pp46-47)
St. Margaret Street, Dunfermline, Fife KY12 7PE
T: 01383 739026

Dunham Massey (pp40-41)
Altrincham, Cheshire WA14 4SJ
T: 0161 941 1025
W: www.nationaltrust.org.uk

Durham Cathedral (pp100-101)
Durham DH1 3EH
T: 01913 864266
W: www.durhamcathedral.co.uk

Eilean Donan Castle (pp88-89)
Dornie – by Kyle of Lochalsh, IV40 8DX, Scotland
T: 01599 555202
W: www.eileandonancastle.com

Fountains Abbey and Studley Royal Water Garden (pp60-61)
Ripon, North Yorkshire HG4 3DY
T: 01765 608888
W: www.fountainsabbey.org.uk

Glamis Castle (pp70-71)
Glamis, Forfar, Angus DD8 1RJ
T: 01307 840393
W: www.glamis-castle.co.uk

Glastonbury Tor (pp38-39)
Glastonbury, Somerset
T: 01985 843600
W: www.nationaltrust.org.uk

Hadrian's Wall Path National Trail (pp68-69)
Hadrian's Wall, Hexham, Northumberland
T: 01912 691600
W: www.nationaltrail.co.uk/hadrianswall

Hampton Court Palace (pp20-21)
East Molesey, Surrey KT8 9AU
T: 0870 752 7777
W: www.hrp.org.uk

Harlech Castle (p32-33)
Castle Square, Harlech, Gwynedd LL46 2YH
T: 01766 780552

Ilford Manor (pp42-43)
Bradford on Avon, Wiltshire
T: 01225 863146
W: www.ilfordmanor.co.uk

Iona Abbey (pp82-83)
Isle of Iona, Argyll PA76 6SN
T: 01681 700474

Little Moreton Hall (pp108-109)
Congleton, Cheshire CW12 4SD
T: 01260 272018
W: www.nationaltrust.org.uk

**Margam Abbey and Stones
Museum** (pp28-29)
Margam, Port Talbot, Neath Port Talbot,
W: www.visitwales.com

Paxton House (pp50-51)
Paxton, Berwick-upon-Tweed, Borders TD15 1SZ
T: 01289 386291
W: www.paxtonhouse.com

Penshurst Place and Gardens (pp54-55)
Penshurst, Kent TN11 8DG
T: 01892 870307
W: www.penshurstplace.com

Powis Castle and Garden (pp78-79)
Welshpool, Powys SY21 8RF
T: 01938 551944
W: www.nationaltrust.org.uk

Rockingham Castle (pp30-31, 48-49)
Rockingham, Market Harborough,
Leicestershire LE16 8TH
T: 01536 770240
W: www.rockinghamcastle.com

Royal Pavilion (pp92-93)
Brighton, East Sussex BN1 1EE
T: 01273 290900
W: www.royalpavilion.org.uk

Rievaulx Abbey (pp104-105)
Rievaulx Abbey, North Yorkshire YO62 5LB
T: 01904 601974
W: www.english-heritage.org.uk

Rutland Water Nature Reserve (pp62-63)
Two miles from Oakham Station, Rutland,
Leicestershire
T: 01572 770651
W: www.rutlandwater.org.uk

Scotney Castle Garden and Estate (pp36-37)
Lamberhurst, Royal Tunbridge Wells, Kent TN2 8JN
T: 01892 891081
W: www.nationaltrust.org.uk

Sheffield Park Garden (pp90-91)
Sheffield Park, Uckfield, East Sussex TN22 3QX
T: 01825 790231
W: www.nationaltrust.org.uk

Stourhead House and Garden (pp16-17)
Stourton, Warminster, Wiltshire BA12 6QD
T: 01747 841152
W: www.nationaltrust.org.uk

The Peak District (pp64-65)
T: 01433 650953
W: www.visitpeakdistrict.com

Tolquhon Castle (pp58-59)
Tarves, Ellon, Aberdeenshire, AB41 7LP
T: 01651 851286

York Minster (pp26-27)
Deangate, York, North Yorkshire Y01 7HH
T: 01904 557216
W: www.yorkminster.org

Image Acknowledgements

Angel, David	18
Barnes, Dennis	46
Bell, Graham	28
Brent, Martin	12, 26, 35, 38, 72
Britainonview.com	16, 20, 22, 23, 32, 34, 43, 50, 56, 58, 78, 83, 88, 92, 98, 99, 112
East Midlands Tourism / Bosworth, Daniel	64
Edwards, Rod	24, 68, 70, 76, 84
Guy, VK / Guy, Paul	100
Hardley, Dennis	66
Libera, Pawel	14, 74
McCormick – McAdam	104
McKinlay, Doug	102
Miller, John	80
Novelli, Alan	40, 108
Pleavin, Tony	10, 48, 52, 62,
Pritchard, Grant	31
Rasmussen, Ingrid	42, 86, 87, 97, 107
Sellman, David	55, 94, 110
Shaw, Ian	8
Taylor, Howard	36
Watson, Richard	4, 44, 60
Woodcock, Jennie	90

All the photographs featured in Heritage Britain are supplied by britainonview.com, the official online image library of VisitBritain.

Britainonview

Quotation Acknowledgements

13   Felicia Hemens (1793-1835), The Poetical Works of Mrs. Hemans, Kessinger Publishing (30 June, 2004)

30   Sir Edward Coke (1552-1634), The Third Part of the Institutes of the Laws of England (1628) ch. 73, p. 162

47   George Crabbe (1754-1832), The Borough (1810) Letter 2 'The Church' 1.11

54   Sir Thomas More (1529-1532), The Re-enchantment of Everyday Life, Harper Perennial (9 April, 1997)

75   William Butler Yeats (1865-1939), source unconfirmed

82   Alix Brown, This is the Day: Readings and Meditations from the Iona Community,
         Neil Paynter, ed. Wild Goose Publications

93   Noel Coward (1899-1973), source unconfirmed

96   Jane Austen (1775-1817), Northanger Abbey (1818) ch. 10

106   Anne Seward (1862-1948), source unconfirmed

Particular thanks go to Louise Hume of the Brighton Royal Pavilion, Libraries and Museums and
Lorna Rae of Iona Books.